The Natural World of
THE TEXAS BIG THICKET

Photographs by BLAIR PITTMAN

INTRODUCTION BY WILLIAM A. OWENS

Texas A&M University Press   COLLEGE STATION AND LONDON

Library of Congress Cataloging in Publication Data

Pittman, Blair, 1937–
    The natural world of the Texas Big Thicket.

    (The Louise Lindsey Merrick Texas environment series; no. 2)
    1. Natural history—Texas—Big Thicket National Park. 2. Big
Thicket National Park, Tex. I. Owens, William A., 1905– II. Title.
III. Series.
QH105.T4P56   500.9764'157   78-6369
ISBN 0-89096-061-5

Manufactured in the United States of America
FIRST EDITION

For Tink and Troy

Contents

Acknowledgments

My photography in the Big Thicket grew out of an appreciation of the outdoors and of nature. My first trip to the Thicket was in 1969. In the years since, I have made many lasting friends there who have given their hospitality, their time, their knowledge and encouragement.

I quickly learned that to know the land is to know the people who live there. Some showed me their part of the Thicket, others helped with detailed identifications. All these friends, together, made this book possible. I was in the right place at the right time.

I would like to express my appreciation to the Big Thicket Association, particularly Alice Cashen and Maxine Johnston, Bill and Annalou Brett, Jude and Johnnie Lea Hart, Dolly and Lige Hoffman, Harold Nicholas, Roy Hamric, John Tveten, and Archer Fullinghim.

Special thanks are due Geraldine Watson, who gave me so much of her knowledge and valuable time, and I. C. Eason, who made possible photography in the Neches River Bottom.

I would also like to thank the National Geographic Society, especially Robert E. Gilka, senior assistant editor, and Robert S. Patton, picture editor, for their help during my four-year assignment covering the Big Thicket.

Exploring the Big Thicket

The Big Thicket in Southeast Texas is a wilderness area that provides the public an opportunity to explore the solitude of woods and streams and the scientist a laboratory for study of a unique combination of plant systems ranging from sub-tropical to semi-arid. The Big Thicket Museum at Saratoga is the logical place for a stranger to start the many hikes he will need before he can say he knows this remaining part of the Texas wild. Though not at the center of the original area it is in the part now thought of as the traditional Thicket. It is also within walking distance of the Lance Rosier Unit and the upper floodplains of the Pine Island Bayou. On his own he can follow a trail through palmetto-hardwood flats and get an instant feeling of trees and vines and palmettos typical of that plant community, enough to know that he should get some instructions at the museum and start over again.

The museum is a do-it-yourself remodeling of an abandoned school. The exhibits inside appear to have been arranged with the same do-it-yourself casualness. This appearance comes not from lack of knowledge or interest but from the desire of the Big Thicket Association to cram as much of the natural world and the cultural world of the area into this small space as it will hold. Members are aware that because of inroads from all sides time is running out for the preservation of both worlds. The museum is scientifically oriented to the diverse fauna and flora, in plant associations unmatched in North America, in rare combinations that justify setting land aside. It is less scientifically but as knowledgeably oriented to the culture of a people who settled in the thickets more than a century ago and kept their culture relatively unchanged. Space is provided for mounted specimens of plant and animal life. Exhibits of Big Thicket paintings and photographs, including some from this book, crowd the wall spaces. Costumes and tools and dozens of other items show how the people lived. Administered and guided by the National Park Service, the Big Thicket Museum attempts to coordinate its programs with those of the federal agency.

The part of the wilderness preserved is not one area but a collection of areas. The stranger needs a guide to help him find an area and to help him know and appreciate what he is seeing. Since it has no single feature like a geyser or a waterfall, a mesa or a peak—the elevation ranges from 5 feet above sea level at the southern edge and 325 at the northern—the visitor must make his own focus on trees and plants, swamps and streams, from cathedral forests to rare orchids to a tiny sundew carnivore dining on an ant. The museum recommends guides, some of them Big Thicket natives who are as aware of local lore as they are of pitcher plants, fire ants, armadillos. The visitor will also need transportation. The Big Sandy Unit, for instance, interesting in its own right, more interesting because it adjoins the Alabama-Coushatta Indian Reservation, is some fifty miles from the museum. Along most roads the guide will be able to point out a rotting log house or corn crib or a local historical scene that will link the present to the past of the first white men to come in.

These early settlers were of pioneer stock, their ancestry in England, Scotland, Wales, with a dominant strain the Scotch-Irish from Northern Ireland. A kind of outer fringe of the great western migrations, they began reaching Southeast Texas about 1820, at the time that Mexico was in revolt against Spain, at the time that political control of Texas was passing from Spain to Mexico. Some of these pioneers were descendants of families who had traveled from frontier to frontier from Virginia across Kentucky and Tennessee, down through Arkansas and Northern Louisiana. Others came from Southern Virginia and the Carolinas, some following the southern highlands, some the southern lowlands. Census records show that the largest numbers were born in Tennessee, Alabama, and Mississippi. Whichever route they took they were chiefly Southern in their customs, language, lore, independence, and fundamentalist beliefs, and they came not because of one land promotion or another but because they were lured by word-of-mouth accounts.

Like their pioneer ancestors they traveled as they could, a few with a slave or two in wagon trains, a few in oxcarts, the majority riding horses or walking. Like earlier pioneers they took with them what they could but the essentials were gun, ax, and iron pot for cooking. Those who had them carried Bibles, the source of fundamentalist faith even for those who could not read.

For some the route lay directly across the Neutral Ground, an area long in dispute between the United States and Spain, a no-man's-land inhabited chiefly by renegades. They braved the dangers and came to the edge of what the Indians called the Big Woods, a tract of about three and a half million acres stretching as far north as the Spanish settlement at San Augustine, south to the Gulf coastal plain, west to the Trinity River. Settlers called it what it appeared to be, the Big Thicket. Indians, some living in scattered villages, some in isolated cabins, traveled the streams and hunting trails. As they had moved west, trying to keep ahead of white men, Indian encounters were rare and usually peaceful. Not until the Alabama-Coushatta Indian Reservation was established were they able to preserve for themselves a fraction of what in the early nineteenth century they had considered their own. The only other inhabitants when the whites came were renegades who had escaped there when the United States decided to clean up the Neutral Ground.

Anglos, as they came to be called, traveled in groups; they settled in groups. As on earlier frontiers they named their communities by adding *settlement* to proper names like Drake or Sandy Creek. Many of the people were kin by blood or marriage. Another kinship, perhaps with stronger bonds, was in the white spirituals they sang in log cabin meetings, the British ballads with which they whiled away hours at work or in the glow of a light'ood knot flame, or in fiddle tunes that still carried the droning sound of bagpipes.

They looked for wood and water and land with growths of pine and hardwoods and an underbase of limestone they had found good for crops in Georgia and Alabama. In the upper reaches of the Big Thicket they found the rolling land, the pines and hardwoods, enough to make them feel at home, and a few small prairies easily cleared for planting. Game was plentiful, small game, large game including deer and bear, and razorback hogs, invaders that had apparently escaped from early Spanish explorers. They found places they liked and took up squatters' rights. Land claims could be proved up later. They cleared land and built houses, barns, smokehouses, all of logs at first. Houses were of hewed logs chinked with split timbers and daubed with clay, as were the stick-and-dirt chimneys. They were generally of two kinds: the smaller a one-pen with a shed room at the back, the larger a two-pen with a hall, called a dog-trot, in between, with sometimes a porch across the front and a shed room at the back forming an L. Barns and smokehouses were pole pens. All were built to last but most eventually sank back into the earth. Only the Richardson house on Turkey Creek survives as an example within the preserve boundaries and it was built in 1925 as a replica of a house built on the same spot in 1855.

These settlements were small, isolated, as isolated as any in a Kentucky hollow, more than any in a bend of the Alabama River. Cut off from books and schools, children grew up unable to read or write, children of the woods, skilled in the ways of wolf and panther and in the use of the gun. Boys and girls, like the men and women, worked in the fields and fought the encroachment of the wilderness. They built fences to keep out cattle and hogs. They dug and hoed and complained when heavy rains set out the weeds and grass they had hacked up the day before.

Interaction between place and people eventually left a mark on both, an impact that was strong on those who remained in the upper Thicket, stronger on those who ventured south into the lower Thicket. There the rainfall was heavier—up to sixty inches a year—the land swampy, the vegetation a tangle of trees and vines and underbrush. Bald cypress trees hung with gray Spanish moss gave a sense of mystery; the womanlike scream of a panther dug deep in the bones.

Inner reaches were to be avoided except by the fearless or the fugitive. These went farther and farther in, into regions where green-brown marshes covered the land, where streams flowed brown as tobacco juice, where jungle growth shut out the sun and left green shadows dark and forbidding.

For a generation or two their impact on the Thicket was slight. Men and women lived out their lives doing what they could, and that was little beyond their own house and patch of ground and there they lost almost as much as they gained. Buildings sank back into the earth. Homesites disappeared in the rapid renewal of nature, and there is little to show for the struggle. There are no historical markers within the preserve to commemorate either a man or a building. Yet there are names carried forward in local history and lore, and in the names they lent to streams and roads and settlements.

Lumber companies were the first major invaders. The relatively small migration before the Civil War increased rapidly as people left destitute in the older South crossed into Texas as if they were crossing into a promised land. Towns began circling the Thicket. Lumber was needed for buildings and for crossties for railroads stretching south and west. The Big Thicket had what seemed an inexhaustible supply of virgin pine and hardwoods. Lumber men built sawmills and cut logging roads, each an invasion of forests as they had been. Timber workers cut big trees and let them fall where they would. Smaller trees that might have been replacements were crushed into the ground. What had been a high canopy began to disappear. An ecological system had been upset. Left to the lumbering methods of the time, all but the most inaccessible parts of the Thicket would have vanished. This with the unwitting aid of Big Thicket people. Men had left farming and hunting for jobs that would run out when the timber was gone. Had they foreseen what might happen, they could hardly raise a voice against their employers.

New invaders came in with the discovery of oil at Spindletop south of Beaumont in 1901. The pace of life quickened; new life styles came in. In two years the population of Beaumont jumped from nine thousand to fifty thousand. In the same year the discovery of oil at Saratoga changed a small resort village into a boom town of tents and rough-cut lumber. Sour Lake, a larger resort town, with the discovery of oil went to ten thousand almost overnight. Batson's Prairie had only five scattered houses in October, 1903, when the discovery well came in. By the next January the population was estimated at ten thousand.

The impact on land and people still cannot be fully measured. Men who had lost out on farms or in cities, men who had worked for a dollar a day in Big Thicket timber, overnight found jobs in oil fields at three dollars a day. Because they worked twelve hours on, twelve hours off, they wanted to move closer to the fields and bring their families with them. Land had to be cleared. Lumber had to be cut for houses, oil derricks, cypress tanks, crossties for more railroads.

Though on a smaller scale, oil proved as devastating as lumbering. Oil was black gold and men were willing to do to the land what was necessary to get it. They got more than they could use or sell and let wells gush out of control till oil flowed over land and down ravines and streams, blackening the earth as it went. Natural gas, clear and odorless as air, sometimes flowed as freely. Trillions of cubic feet of poisonous gas rose unchecked in the air and settled in low places, killing whatever breathed it. Damage had been done before flares were developed for burning it. Salt water continues to be a troublesome and destructive by-product of drilling. Before rice farmers took oil men to court, it flowed down streams and bayous and collected in lakes so salty that no plants would grow, lakes that soon became stark graveyards with broken trunks and cypress knees rising like gravestones. The market for oil grew, the search for oil spread. Wildcatters cut roads and drilled wells farther and farther into the Thicket. Whether they found oil or not, they left clearings with ragged edges, scars that might take nature a generation to cover over.

A few years of intense activity and the booms were over. Wells that had gushed now had to be pumped, and the number gradually declined. Boomers went on to newly discovered fields, leaving behind skeletons of derricks and tanks and piles of rusting pipes. Not all the boomers went. The Big Thicket got hold of some and they stayed, soon to become indistinguishable from any of the other Big Thicket people.

Through the years, farming, logging, drilling increased till by 1938 forested acres had dwindled to a few hundred thousand and the pace was increasing. When final denudation of the best seemed inevitable, a new movement came into being, fostered by a breed of people who called themselves environmentalists, people who had no reason to fear or hate the wilderness and many reasons to love and save it. Regionally centered at first, the movement became national and eventually powerful. In Southeast Texas it found its voice early in the East Texas Big Thicket Association, forerunner of the Big Thicket Association. It was a small voice, but a nagging, persistent one directed at vulnerable targets: corporations and their officials who had neither personal nor emotional involvement in the Big Thicket.

World War II over, the corporations were larger, their claims bolder, their demands on natural resources greater. Oil companies cut more and more swaths for their pipelines and service roads. Lumber companies widened and extended their logging roads to accommodate newer, heavier, more destructive machinery. The wood pulp industry expanded to meet increasing demands for newsprint as well as demands for an ever-widening number of paper products. Before the war the lumber industry had been largely local. Now it became national and international as conglomerates moved in. Before the war cutting had been largely selective and destructive enough. After the war selective cutting was replaced by clearcutting wherever practical, with the land bulldozed clean and planted with pine trees in rows for the convenience of harvesting machines. Clearcutting took all or most of the hardwoods and left no shelter for animals, no plant life to sustain them. Large-scale devastation had set in. In part to silence protests of environmentalists, in part perhaps because of a feeling for the Big Thicket, the lumber industry endorsed proposals that nine areas with a total of 35,500 acres be set aside for a national monument as recommended by the National Park

Service in 1967. This suggestion was rejected by the environmentalists.

The Big Thicket Association and their friends had in mind saving a large block of land, but they were too late. Towns had been built. Highways and feeder roads crisscrossed it. In the end they had to settle for 84,550 acres, divided into twelve widely scattered units. On October 11, 1974, President Gerald Ford signed into law a bill authorizing a Big Thicket National Preserve, thus sealing a compromise between House and Senate arrived at under the shadow of Watergate. The Big Thicket National Preserve was the first designated national preserve administered by the National Park Service. The Corps of Engineers was later called upon to acquire land for the Park Service.

The approved acquisition has been accomplished in most units but not without problems. To many local residents conservation was first a strange word, then a dirty word, and finally a word to be feared. They would have to give up their land and the timber on it. Others simply sold their timber to lumber companies. Some tracts were clearcut though the land had been designated for preservation. Plans for housing developments and trailer camps were reported by landowners and property values became inflated. Though prices offered were often higher than market value, some owners refused to sell.

Before preserve boundaries were published, several landowners sold timber to lumber companies. The tracts could be saved from destruction only by purchasing before contract deadlines. The southern pine beetle invaded several preserve units and the Texas Forest Service invoked the Forest Pest Control Act requiring what came close to wholesale destruction of the Beech Creek Unit. In despair, conservationists pled for money and for use of a procedure called "declaration of taking" in order to save endangered tracts. Thanks to close cooperation among the National Park Service, the Corps of Engineers, the Big Thicket Association, and Congressional Appropriations and Interior committees, most of the areas were preserved intact.

Some residents were angry enough to cut trees for spite or to refuse access to government appraisers with threats of bodily harm. Much of this resistance was due to fear of change. Now major decisions have been made and published, preserve boundaries have been clearly marked, and destruction on preserve-designated property may have ended. There are flickerings of local pride in what has been preserved and in the national attention the Big Thicket has received. It can be assumed that even those who fought hardest against the preserve will realize that the Thicket way of life they knew has to come to an end and that no matter how hard they try to hold onto it for their children it will never again be the same. The idea may come slowly but it will come: a Big Thicket preserved in all its aspects is a viable link with the past.

The struggle has been long and expensive but the units are safe in the hands of the National Park Service, twelve of them, the largest covering some 25 thousand acres, the longest the Upper and Lower Neches River units with corridors stretching eighty miles from Town Bluff to Beaumont. Each was selected because it contains a distinct plant association. Each is different enough from the others to require visits to all if one is to appreciate fully the wide range of plant communities within the preserve. Unless the visitor is also a trained botanist he will need a guide to point out important specimens that in size and color may seem unimportant.

Few straight lines bound these units. Surveyors and mapmakers had to follow crooked streams and crooked trails. The shapes are as irregular as nature itself. At the same time this nature affords examples of perfection that satisfy the universal desire for form. A leaf, a petal, a cone may demonstrate perfect symmetry but, taken together in the lushness of the Big Thicket, they tumble into formlessness. A perfectly shaped orchid may have to be untangled from grass for the perfection to be perceived.

Most of the units were distinctive enough to early settlers to have been given folk names like Big Sandy Creek, Hickory Creek, Beech Creek, Loblolly, Pine Island Bayou, Jack Gore Baygall. Jack Gore was a settler who lent his name to a watery blemish on the earth, an extended bog, highly acid in nature, matted with debris from moss and ferns, rimmed by a heavy growth of underbrush. Each unit contains several plant communities but not in all possible combinations. As the western-most extension of the Southern Mixed Forest, many of the plants may be found across the South as far as the Everglades or the Okefenokee Swamp, but not all of them. Such northern trees as beech and maple unexplainably grow along Big Thicket streams. Though the western edge of the Big Thicket is some hundreds of miles from the desert, semi-arid plants like varieties of cactus and yucca sink roots deep in sandy-land areas. Such is the diversity of the soil that these semi-arid plants may be found only yards away from lush sub-tropical growth. This diversity is emphasized in the names Geraldine Watson has listed for the major plant communities: prairies, palmetto-hardwood flats, stream floodplains, sandylands, acid bog–baygall, longleaf pine uplands, pine savannah wetlands, beech-magnolia-pine associations. Even these namings are not enough to suggest the orchids, grasses, carnivorous plants that make a part of the ground cover.

In acres as well as in plant communities these units form only a select part of the Big Thicket. In the thousands of acres under private ownership plant communities exist that should be preserved. It is encouraging that in recent years some private preserves have been created. In both private and public preserves renewal is under way, in the public aided by the skill of conservation experts. Where fires set by lightning once kept spaces open for ground plants, fires set by Park Service employees burn off the invaders.

Units in the wetter areas are still in a wilderness state, heavily wooded, heavily tangled with vines. Typical scenes are marked by closeness and quiet and peace seemingly disturbed by nothing more threatening than a bird call. Yet in this closeness there is such an infinite variety of form and color that the eye is constantly in the process of selecting.

The peace that seems to pervade these wildernesses is, however, as illusory between non-human as between man and man. It is a constant battleground between predator and prey in the eternal struggle for survival, the struggle that also helps to maintain a natural balance, a struggle that in the preserve is aided by man when he sees the need to step in. Frogs eat insects, snakes eat frogs, snakes, cannibals, eat other snakes, alligators gobble up anything from minnows to minks and bigger. Silences are broken by the agonized screams from rabbits caught by bobcats and coyotes. Screeching birds chase crows from their nests. Squirrels chatter noisily at blue jays trying to steal their young. But not all the conflict is noisy. Spiders eat flies quietly. Wasps eat spiders as quietly.

The Park Service and environmentalists know that in such fragile areas people must be taught conservation rules and strict adherence to them—taught against taking more of anything than they can use, taught to plant a tree where one grew before, taught against killing because of old fears, old superstitions, against killing for the sake of killing. They must be taught to pass a moccasin or copperhead on the trail and not yield to the urge to kill. Let a poisonous snake go? Yes. A deadly one? Yes. Suffer the fear and let it lie? Yes.

This wilderness is precious, and a new consciousness is required. We must learn that a flower dug beside a trail is not likely to bloom with such beauty in a home garden—if at all. Even if one did, constant plucking would put any flower on the endangered list. We must learn to stay on pathways, knowing that too many spread-out tracks will leave the ground packed and bare.

The ivory-billed woodpecker is a constant reminder of what can happen. Once plentiful, it is now extinct or so nearly so that thousands of watchers have failed to catch a glimpse. The same could happen to his cousin, the pileated, still to be seen in reassuring numbers. It has already happened to the colony of roseate spoonbills nearby, victims of accidental spraying. It could happen to the egrets, or to any of the rare birds passing through on this major flyway.

In their awareness of the natural world of the Big Thicket, visitors should reserve some appreciation for the customs and lore of Big Thicket people. Many of the settlements were remarkably isolated until after World War II. There was electricity in the towns but not outside. There were no radios, no television sets, and very few newspapers. In their isolation people told and retold their folk history: of the hardships their ancestors endured coming to the Thicket, of local characters and bloody feuds, of hunting trips for bear and panther and razorback hogs. It was oral history, rich, told in a language ancient in sound, sprinkled with made-up words and words as old as Anglo-Saxon itself.

Entertainment was in ballad singing and, where religious belief or lack of belief permitted, square dancing to fiddle and guitar, to tunes out of the frontier—"Cattle in the Canebrake" and "Hell among the Year-lings." In log cabins lighted only with the flame of a pitch pine knot people sang ballads that stretched back to Shakespeare's time and ear-lier, songs of lords and ladies, ballads of love and murder and ghosts at night returning.

The museum is on the right track for preserving Big Thicket culture. At night during retreats, when exploring nature is curtailed, visitors are urged to take part in story telling, ballad singing, and stomping their feet to the music of fiddle and guitar. What happens is a kind of sprawling entertainment and catch-as-catch-can education. Intensive collecting is essential at once. More formal participation must be provided, especially for those who come singly or in small groups from great distances. More extensive collections of photographs and artifacts, with special empha-sis on the impact of the oil fields, would help. For the intangibles like the sound of a voice, the flash of a look, the lonesomeness of a ballad, video tapes would be the answer—tapes to be made while those who remem-ber the past can still perform.

Blair Pittman spent ten years or so inside the preserve and out, searching for his own natural world of the Big Thicket. With the patience of an artist he stalked flowers, animals, reptiles, and waited for the right moment, the right light before he pressed the release. His patience was rewarded with photographs in some instances realistic enough to be used for identification, in some, impressionistic enough to be wholly sat-isfying as photographic art. Some in their underlying statement go be-yond either. The sequence of the snake swallowing the frog, for instance, is a chilling reminder that in nature there has to be both predator and prey. Sympathy rises for the fawn, beautiful and defenseless in a world of predators. The alligator relieves the fierceness of jaws and teeth a little by what appears to be a smile.

The eye of the camera sees what it sees. The vision of the artist photographer determines the focus. Blair Pittman let his vision range widely over the Big Thicket and the pictures in this book provide a record not likely to be repeated.

WILLIAM A. OWENS

The Natural World of
THE TEXAS BIG THICKET

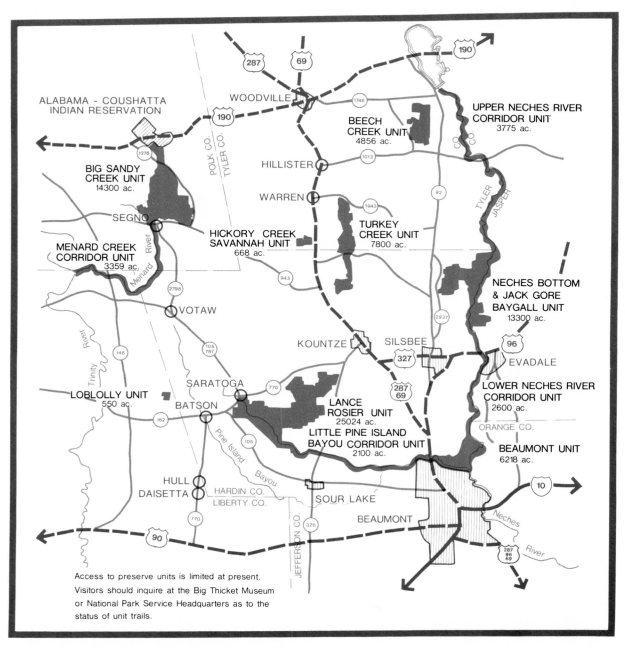

ALABAMA - COUSHATTA
INDIAN RESERVATION

WOODVILLE

BEECH
CREEK UNIT
4856 ac.

UPPER NECHES RIVER
CORRIDOR UNIT
3775 ac.

HILLISTER

BIG SANDY
CREEK UNIT
14300 ac.

WARREN

SEGNO

HICKORY CREEK
SAVANNAH UNIT
668 ac.

TURKEY
CREEK UNIT
7800 ac.

MENARD CREEK
CORRIDOR UNIT
3359 ac.

NECHES BOTTOM
& JACK GORE
BAYGALL UNIT
13300 ac.

VOTAW

KOUNTZE

SILSBEE

EVADALE

LOBLOLLY UNIT
550 ac.

SARATOGA

BATSON

LANCE
ROSIER UNIT
25024 ac.

LITTLE PINE ISLAND
BAYOU CORRIDOR UNIT
2100 ac.

LOWER NECHES RIVER
CORRIDOR UNIT
2600 ac.

ORANGE CO.

BEAUMONT UNIT
6218 ac.

HULL
DAISETTA

HARDIN CO.
LIBERTY CO.

SOUR LAKE

BEAUMONT

JEFFERSON CO.

POLK CO.
TYLER CO.

TYLER
JASPER

Access to preserve units is limited at present.
Visitors should inquire at the Big Thicket Museum
or National Park Service Headquarters as to the
status of unit trails.

Map 1. Big Thicket Preserve units and surrounding area.

Early morning fog

Hardwood floodplain, Big Sandy Unit

Golden silk spider

Rattan vine

"Tight-eye" thicket

Palmetto frond and sun rays

Razorback hog

Detail of palmetto

Baygall near Alligator Grass Lake, reflecting sphagnum moss, sawgrass, and tupelo trees

Tupelo tree and sawgrass

Sweet gum with cork wings

Overleaf: Thunderstorm

Wasp feeding on water spider

Water snake

Dragonfly on bitterweed

Tiger swallowtail and wild azalea

Damselfly

Lichen and fungi growing on log on forest floor

Indian pipe

Death angel

Fly agaric

Fly agaric below fallen tree

Young whitetail deer

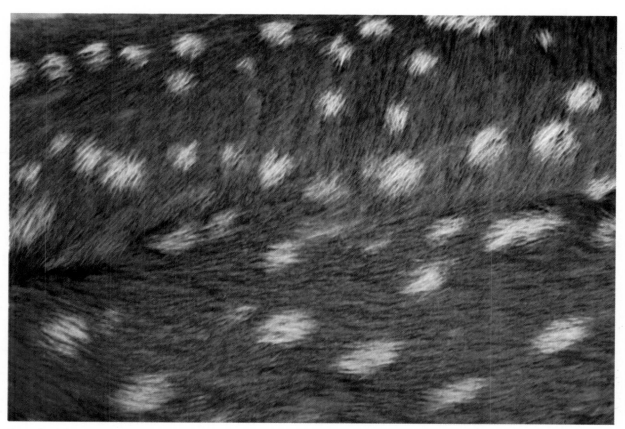

Detail of fawn's spots

Whitetail fawn

Water lily, Grass Lake

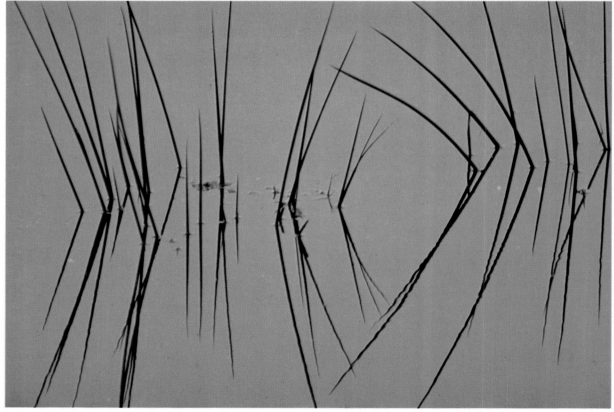

Reeds, Grass Lake

Great egret landing

Young egrets in nest

Great egret and young

American alligator

Alligator (profile)

Baygall

Overleaf: Female wood duck and ducklings

Female wood duck

Backwater slough and duckweed

Young bullfrog in duckweed

Slider turtles in duckweed

Western ribbon snake devouring green tree frog

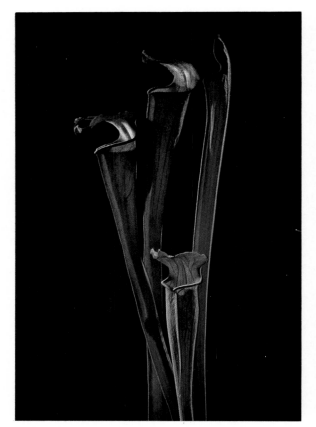

Pitcher plant

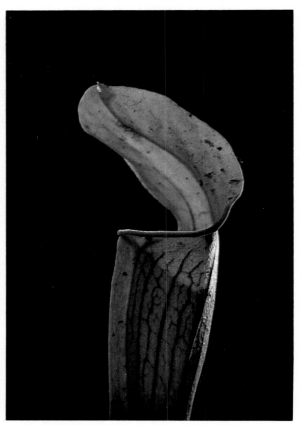

Pitcher plant

Detail of pitcher plant and moth

Life cycle of pitcher plants

Ant trapped in sundew leaf

Dwarf butterwort

Detail of butterwort

Bladderwort, showing body
of plant under water

Floating bladderwort

Baygall with bladderworts

Yellow-fringed orchid and cinnamon fern

Yellow-fringed orchid

Nodding ladies' tresses

Grass-pink orchid

Yellow-fringed orchid and pitcher plant

Pitcher plants after fire

Hercules club or toothache tree

Sun through trees in Jack Gore Baygall

Phlox

Yellow coreopsis

Field of wildflowers (phlox and coreopsis)

Rose gentian

Pineywoods lily

Jack-in-the-pulpit

Widow's tear

72

Sunflowers

Louisiana iris

Iris leaves and water-shield

Spring shower along Village Creek

Raindrop on sweet-gum leaf

Water elm and cypress in the Neches River bottom

Cypress and tupelo in backwater slough, Neches River bottom

Giant oak

Beech-tree branches and leaves

Beech tree on Village Creek

Red oak leaves

Nine-banded armadillo

Canebrake rattler

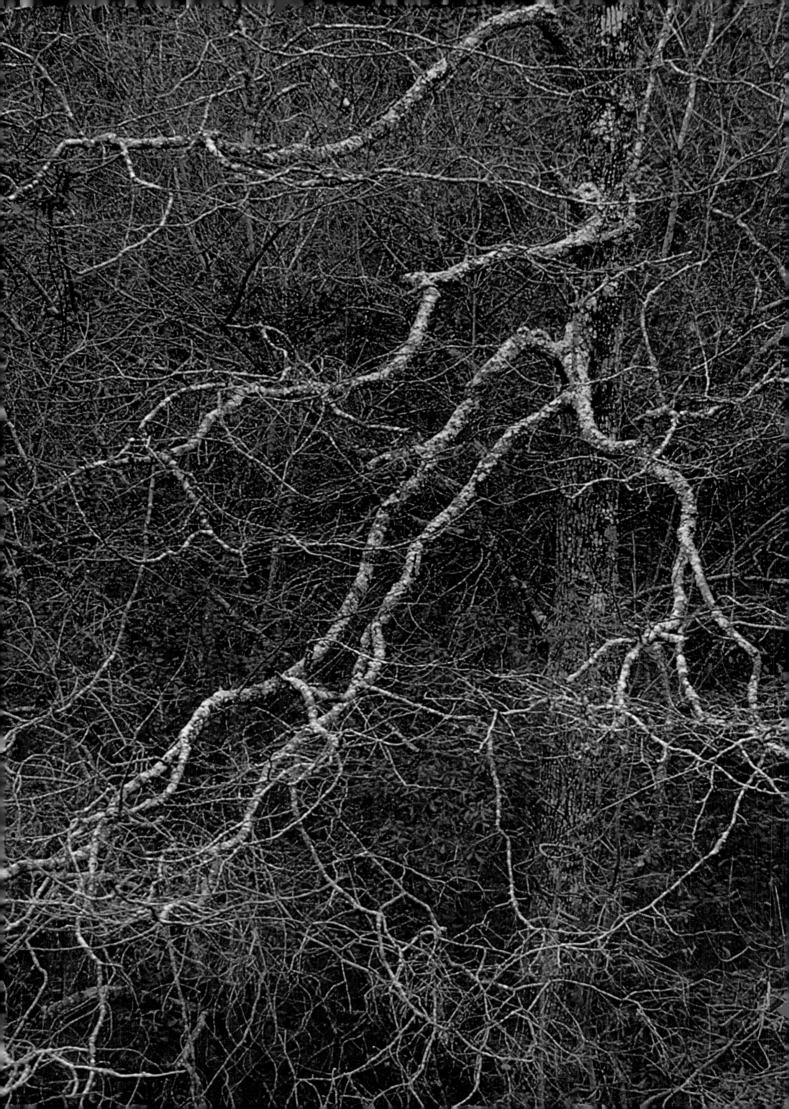

Sycamore and sycamore balls

Oak in winter

Overleaf: Sun through leaves in Jack Gore Baygall

Dogwood in bloom

Raindrops on pine needles

Grass and sun reflecting on pond

Morning fog on Village Creek

Dawn on Village Creek

Morning fog on Village Creek

Water oak and Spanish moss, Village Creek

Overleaf: Village Creek and morning fog

The Photographer's Notes

As in any natural or wilderness area, nature balances itself in the Big Thicket. Here it is eat or be eaten, adapt or disappear. There are no victories, only survival.

Nature has developed a system depending on availability, opportunity, and appetite. Plants, mammals, birds, reptiles, insects, amphibians, and fishes have each evolved a special skill. Some are poisonous, some quick, some camouflaged. Others are keener of sight or smell. For many, survival depends on production of great numbers of their species to ensure their continuation. Within the life-giving food chain, the fauna and flora keep themselves in balance. But this balance is delicate and works only so long as no outside intrusion upsets the relationships.

It disturbs me that man has found it necessary to tamper with such a finely tuned system. At the same time, I do not believe that man or industry has intended to jeopardize the existence of the Big Thicket. The Thicket just happened to get caught up in the machine age, the population explosion, and the twentieth century in general. Man has a tendency to think only of what we call progress. We sometimes overlook the natural world, valuing only what we can measure: growth rate, yield of pine or rice per acre, miles of pipeline or utility lines, pounds of growth on livestock, or barrels of oil per day.

Until recent years only a handful of scientists were aware of the unique botanical diversity of the Big Thicket. Their studies have continued to uncover new and rare species of plant life. Four of North America's five genera of insectivorous plants, some three hundred species of birds, around forty species of orchids, twenty-six species of ferns, and many rare and endangered species cling to existence in the 84,550 acres set aside as the Big Thicket National Preserve.

Now that the people of America have learned what the Big Thicket is and what it stands for, they have spoken up for their heritage to be preserved and protected for the future.

Frontispiece   The flat terrain and slow-moving waters of Pine Island Bayou promote the growth of cypress, palmetto, and Spanish moss. There is a sense of timelessness and promise here in the Thicket's early morning mist.

page 27   Many chilly pre-dawn mornings I met a charter pilot to explore the Big Thicket from the air. As we flew over the Village Creek floodplain, the morning fog rose with the morning sun.

page 28   Sweet gum and water oak form a canopy above the Big Sandy Creek floodplain. The shade inhibits the growth of brushy plants, leaving an open expanse of forest floor. Rattan vines and golden silk spiders flourish in the dim, misty light.

page 29   At the edge of the floodplain the canopy of trees thins and increased sunlight causes a dense tangle of vines and brushy vegetation. Early pioneers called this growth "tight-eye" thicket, a corruption from the original Indian word, "ti ti." This heavy undergrowth is said to be so dense that a rattlesnake has to crawl through it backwards.

pages 30–31   Along Pine Island Bayou the terrain is flat and the water moves sluggishly. Frequent and prolonged flooding allows the palmetto to dominate. Some reach a height of twenty feet. Razorback hogs find the moist flats good for wallow holes. Known locally as "rooters," these hogs are ferocious fighters when cornered. Armed with ivory tusks and a powerful head, they have been known to charge a horse and rider and lift them off the ground.

pages 32–33   From sweet-bay magnolia trees, red bay, and gallberry holly trees these wet boggy areas derive the name "baygalls." Baygalls are topographical depressions in the process of filling with organic debris. Over a long period of time decomposition forms an acid humus. The water is not stagnant but moves slowly. I used a wide-angle lens for a panoramic view showing sphagnum moss and tupelo trees reflected in the water. Sawgrass (actually a sedge) growing at the base of a tupelo tree and leaves floating on the dark water form this detailed composition of a baygall.

The growths along the sweet-gum branches, or "cork wings," are a natural bark formation.

pages 34–35   Summer thunderstorms are a common occurrence. The annual rainfall in the Big Thicket is around sixty inches.

pages 36–37   Looking more like a jungle river than a Big Thicket creek, Big Sandy's banks overhang with yaupon, black gum, native azalea, and arrowwood viburnam.

The outsized wasp is usually the winner against spiders. Wasps, birds, and some other spiders help control spider populations, while the spiders help control the insect population.

A diamond-backed water snake cruises for an evening meal of frog, crayfish, salamander, or fish.

pages 38–39   The dragonfly and the damselfly have much in common. Aquatic insects, they elude most of the enemies of land-oriented insects. But that leaves them prey for fish, frogs, water snakes, and some birds. I followed the dragonfly from one bitterweed plant to another till we arrived at the same place at the same time. Both these insects were found hovering over the sandy soil at the banks of the Neches River.

In early spring the wild azaleas bloom, adding their delicate perfume and color to the season of new beginnings. The tiger swallowtail butterfly aids pollination. I used a long telephoto lens with close-up attachments to get the softness around the butterfly.

pages 40–41   A carpet of dead leaves, broken branches, and dead logs gives life to fungi that grow in the environment of dampness and decay. Indian pipe, a flowering seed-producer, lives on fallen debris. Mushrooms, however, produce spores and may live on living or waste material. The death angel and the fly agaric (both of the amanita family) are poisonous.

Mushrooms can be found most commonly following a rain. The Indian pipe was photographed in late fall.

pages 42–43 The only one of the deer family found in the Big Thicket is the whitetail. They have long been considered a staple of hunters. A friend of mine bottle-fed this fawn. The doe had been killed, and the fawn was raised as a house pet. He was curious about all the cameras but, after sniffing them over, expressed interest only in the clicking sound they occasionally made. After he grew his spikes, he returned to the woods and stayed.

pages 44–45 Alligator Grass Lake is a successional lake. Vegetation and fill are gradually compacting on the bottom; after many years it will eventually become a baygall. Grass Lake is probably an abandoned channel of ancient Village Creek. Camping by Grass Lake, one can easily imagine a much earlier time. As one listens to the primitive drones, chirpings, and occasional secret splash, the twentieth century fades to another time.

Water lilies and reeds add their touch to the perennial beauty of this place.

pages 46–47 Numerous bird rookeries are scattered across the Big Thicket. This one is in the Devil's Pocket. Hundreds of birds overhead keep up a constant racket, chattering and calling. Egrets, great herons, and anhinga nest together in colonies. In these photographs great egrets return to the nest after a food gathering trip, and the great egret guards its young.

Survival here depends on alertness. Dangers are present above and below. Buzzards wait for the weaker young to die. Alligators cruise, waiting for hapless young to fall into the water below. There are usually plenty of predators around when the young try their wings for the first time.

pages 48–49 Alligators still inhabit the Devil's Pocket Baygall. The American alligator is the top of the food chain. He will eat just about anything, suffers from no diseases, and has no enemy other than man. Unless protecting their nest, alligators are nonaggressive, almost timid in nature.

The alligator's appetite and curiosity helped me get these pictures. I sat quietly in the aluminum boat watching several alligators. They were a hundred feet or so away from me, sitting quietly watching me watch them. After several hours of this I got restless and hungry. I reached for my lunch and accidentally knocked over my aluminum camera case. That broke the gators' trance. They swam in to see what was happening. I tossed a piece of bread from my sandwich, and they came to within fifteen feet of the boat. The gators just sat there waiting like dogs to be fed. I alternately took pictures and tossed bits of my sandwich to them. They stayed until I was out of food, then swam away.

pages 50–51   A female wood duck leads her young through the duck-weed of the Devil's Pocket Baygall. Wood ducks usually are found in the ponds and swamps of deep forest. They nest in hollow trees several feet from the ground.

page 52 (top)   After hiding the ducklings in a safe spot, mother wood duck came over to check me out. She came into close range for my long telephoto lens and stopped for me to take pictures, then rejoined the ducklings and swam away with them in single file behind her.

page 53   The bullfrog, camouflaged in the duckweed, demonstrates one of the methods of survival in nature.

Sliders get their name from the way they slide into the water. They are sunning themselves on a partially submerged log covered with duckweed.

pages 54–55   On one of many trips to the Thicket, I was looking for the perfect spider lily. Spider lilies weren't at their best, but I happened upon this scene. The Western ribbon snake had just caught the green tree frog, and I witnessed the sequential event. It was a drama of life and death in microcosm, lasting about thirty minutes.

pages 56–57   Pitcher plants, like other insectivorous plants, are a good example of adaptation. Trapping and digesting insects, they acquire nutrients not available in the nitrogen-poor soil in which they grow. I raised the hood of the pitcher plant to find the moth about to give up climbing against the pull of gravity.

Tiny hairs growing inside some species of the plant make the upward climb even more difficult.

The grasshopper found the carnivorous pitcher plant a good temporary resting place. This photograph shows the plant's life cycle. The yellow-green flower is ready to drop its seeds. The older plant, which has turned brown, has given life of another kind. The hole was made by fly larvae emerging after hatching. The female spirals in, lays eggs, and spirals out again. The eggs hatch in the warmth of decaying insect remains.

pages 58–59

The tiny sundew leaves, clustered at the base of the stem and bloom, exude a sticky substance like tiny dewdrops that traps insects. The close-up of the ant trapped in a sundew leaf (one-quarter inch long) called for bellows and telephoto lens, three strobe units, and slow shutter speed.

The butterwort is the most easily overlooked and least efficient of the insectivorous plants. A light sticky substance covers the leaves. Once trapped, an insect is enwrapped as the leaves fold slowly shut.

pages 60–61

The bladderwort is found throughout the Thicket in still pools, bogs, and baygalls. It floats on the water, supported by star-shaped air sacs. The body of the plant lives underwater and traps small organisms which it holds until deterioration releases the body juices.

I wanted to photograph as much of the bladderwort as possible. By transferring the plant to an aquarium, one can see all parts of the plant, above water, floating on the water, with the main plant body underwater.

pages 62–63

Throughout the year various orchids attain their maximum growth and beauty. Although some orchids are found in drier sandy parts of the Thicket, the yellow-fringed orchid (summer), nodding ladies' tresses (fall), and the grass-pink orchid (early summer) are all found in moist areas.

pages 64–65

Forest fire is as ancient as the forest itself. In her own way nature "prunes" and eliminates species too inflexible for survival. Many of the rare and unusual plants have developed a fire tolerance, and even dependence, that ensures their continuation even in areas where fires are frequent.

A few days after a natural fire sweeps across a pitcher plant bog, plants are stirring with new-found life. These fire-born pitcher plants are several weeks old. They mature and grow rapidly, partly because of the elimination of undesirable competing species.

pages 66–67   I approached Grass Lake at sunset. I was composing a picture of the sedge and the sunset color reflecting on the water when something dove for safety, causing the ripples.

page 68   The strange bark of the Hercules club tree makes it easy to identify. This tree is on the Alabama-Coushatta Indian Reservation. It is also known as the prickly ash or the toothache tree by the Indians, who cut the inner bark to anesthetize an aching tooth.

page 69   Beneath this sun-screening canopy Jack Gore Baygall lies cool and moist.

pages 70–71   A few weeks earlier when I visited this spot along the roadside, there wasn't a wildflower in sight, but this time purple and white phlox along with coreopsis turned the opening into a colorful carpet of nature.

pages 72–73   I was attracted by the bright green fly on the rose gentian. The pastel colors were accentuated because the sun was behind a cloud. For the pineywoods lily I got underneath the plant where the sun was blocked by the body of the plant. The shade-loving jack-in-the-pulpit was photographed after a rain in Jack Gore Baygall. I found the widow's tear with a dewdrop shortly after dawn. The sunflowers were backlighted by the sun in the morning haze. The Louisiana iris was also photographed just following a shower.

pages 74–75   Along the edge of a pond in the Devil's Pocket I was attracted by the combination of vertical lines of iris leaves offset by the circular pattern of water-shield. To keep the reflection of trees present but not dominant, I used a medium telephoto lens to soften the tree images.

After a spring shower is a good time to wander through the

Thicket's fresh clear light and just-washed smells. With the rain still creeping down branches and leaves, the patterns of spring emerge.

pages 76–77   In cypress swamps squirrels strip the shaggy bark for their nests and bird rookeries are common. The tupelos stand along Becky Lake, an oxbow once part of the Neches River or an associated waterway.

Giant live oaks, planted by the first settlers in the Thicket, are found near abandoned homesites dating from the early 1800's. The pattern of beech branches characterizes the forest canopy.

pages 78–79   The beech is my favorite tree. Each branch fans out with a dendritic pattern, reaching far, far out from the trunk. Morning fog on Village Creek accentuates the beech's delicate shape. The Southern red oak adds its own pattern of autumn.

Some things scurry and rustle in the autumn leaves, like the armadillo, common in the Thicket. But others, like the fairly rare canebrake rattlesnake, sit poised and ready to lunge for a meal, silent and lethal.

pages 80–81   Winter in the Big Thicket reveals the bold shape of oak branches on lower Village Creek. The blue-gray light of an overcast day helped separate the color values.

Near Pine Island Bayou the late afternoon silhouette of the sycamore tree accents the curved stem holding each of the balls.

pages 82–83   The light in Jack Gore Baygall works magic. The tree branches and leaves almost blot out the sun, splintering the light rays.

pages 84–85   With much of my photography I take advantage of the natural special effects that nature offers, like the grass along a pond. I exposed for the reflected sparkles on the water.

The flowering dogwood blossoms are short-lived, depending on the weather and the rain. They are graceful, fragrant, and for that short time add an eloquent beauty to the Big Thicket.

Inside the raindrops forest and sun are reflected.

pages 86–87   Pines occur both in pine forests and in association with hardwoods, as in this photograph. Morning fog and a medium

98

telephoto lens join the vertical and horizontal lines but keep them from merging.

Sunrise along the Neches River is a study of clouds and reflections.

pages 88–89   Misty blue dawn comes to Village Creek. As the sun moves higher into the sky the blue turns to gold shining through dripping Spanish moss.

page 90   I wanted to conclude the *Natural World of the Texas Big Thicket* with an optimistic eye toward the future. Daybreak is a time of beginnings, what I call the magic time of the day. Here on Village Creek nature is at her best. The morning dew hangs heavy; the morning fog completes the picture of pristine stillness.